THESE THINGS I PRAY FOR YOU
My Child

By Jessa R. Sexton

These Things I Pray for You: My Child
Copyright © 2013 by Jessa Sexton
ISBN-13: 978-0-9912792-2-7

Cover Design by Brianna Miele & Whitnee Clinard
with photography by Jessa R. Sexton
Book Block Design by Whitnee Clinard
All rights reserved. No part of this publication may be reproduced or transmitted in any form or by any means without written permission of the author.

Published by Hilliard Press
a division of The Hilliard Institute
Franklin, Tennessee
Oxford, England

www.hilliardinstitute.com

Dedication

for my boys, Jack Everett and Jonas Hilliard

(who change ages in this book as I worked on it over a period of time)

and

for June-Girl

(who arrived after I wrote this)

Preface

I've been praying for my sons since before I was ever pregnant, since before I knew they'd be boys. We are pregnant again, and soon there will be a little girl in our family. Getting to know my children has helped me specify those early prayer desires. I don't pray in general anymore, as I know, when I look at them, what I want for them.

As we think of the characteristics and blessings we would pray for our children, or our grandchildren, a knowledge of the word and of The Word—what the dictionary and others say about the word's meaning and intent, and what God's Scriptures say—will make our prayers deeper, give better direction to our hopes. So this study creates that direction to a mother's prayers.

Note that I have placed questions towards the back of the book to further your time of reflection on each chapter. You can use this section alone, in a class setting, or with a group of friends.

Introduction

"Do not be anxious about anything, but in every situation, by prayer and petition, with thanksgiving, present your requests to God." Philippians 4:6

"Devote yourselves to prayer, being watchful and thankful." Colossians 4:2

"Ask and it will be given to you; seek and you will find; knock and the door will be opened to you. For everyone who asks receives; the one who seeks finds; and to the one who knocks, the door will be opened." Matthew 7:7-8

I can worry about how my children will turn out, or I can actively, "in every situation," come before the Lord and ask with boldness for blessings to rain over them.

I choose the latter.

Quotes about this Book

"It's hard as a foster mom to know what to pray for the little souls that pass quickly through my home. Each characteristic talked about in *These Things I Pray for You* was something I could pray over my babies while they are with me and after they leave. I loved how the author brought each characteristic to life with definitions, personal stories, and Bible verses. The prayers at the end of each chapter are prayers I will go back to over and over again, not just for the children in my life but for myself as well."
- *Jessi DeFoor: foster mother, childcare specialist, and friend*

"I think the whole idea of prayer is troublesome, whether for our children or friends or anyone. We say things like, let so-and-so be encouraged...and then stop to think: encouraged to do what? Get good grades in school, avoid bad companions, go to church regularly? Somehow those things, while admirable, never seem to be more than place fillers for the 'real deal.'

"Anyway, my point is that [this book's] list and explanations seem to be far more complete than I could ever dream up in the 20 minutes or so that I might be allotting for prayer for my grandchildren.

"I must also mention that the appeal of the book is in how very well written it is. The author has produced something that I believe has the potential to be a real seller and have lasting benefits to the readers."

- Carolyn Davis: grandmother, retired librarian, avid reader, and friend

"The challenges of raising godly children in a very ungodly world are sobering, overwhelming, and at times even terrifying. What comfort it is to present these precious souls before our Creator knowing He will indeed help us. As a new mom, I've found this collection of prayers for my children to be a real treasure. A thorough compilation and a joy to read, this devotional proves to be insightful and throught-provoking. My prayer life has certainly been enriched having read it, and that directly benefits my children–priceless."

- Heather Prasser: mother, dental hygienist, and friend

"Praying for my grandchild is humbling, soul-searching, and selfless. Jessa's book gives me direction as I seek God's purpose in my life as a praying grandmother."

- Pam Sekulow, grandmother, educator, and friend:

"As a new mom, I often worry about my baby and wonder, 'Am I raising him right? Am I doing all that I can do to bring him up correctly in the way of the Lord?' This book provides excellent guidance for the most helpful way a mother can be active in her child's life: by praying for him or her. As Paul tells us in Philippians 4:6, 'Do not be anxious, but instead-in prayer-present your requests to God.' That is exactly the purpose of this book, and why it is a valuable resource for moms in any stage of life with any parenting style."

— *Emily Waller: mother, technical writer, and cousin*

Table of Contents

Dedication 3
Preface 5
Introduction 7
Philologia 13
Peace 17
Purity 23
Passion 29
Purpose 35
Prosperity 41
Perseverance 47
Companionship 53
Compassion 59
Courage 65
Cleverness 69
Health 73
Humor 79
Happiness 83
Hope 87
Heaven 91
Notes 98
Questions for Reflection 101
Final Note 111
References 113
About the Author 117

Philologia

The Word

As I was making my list of qualities I pray my sons will have instilled in their natures, I decided to ask a friend and mother of three, Denise, what she wanted for her children. "I pray they have a love of learning," she answered. Of course I, professor and research-addict, feel the same way, but it wasn't something I had thought of as a specific prayer request. But I had a problem: "Can you put that into a word beginning with P, C, or H?" I asked. "I have a theme going." Denise laughed at me and said she'd think about it.

So, research-addict that I am, I searched "love of learning" online. My discovery didn't take long in coming: *philologia*.

Philologia is the Greek word for "love of discussion, learning, and literature" ("Philogia"). Perfect. And how much more perfect that I found the word that defines this quality while I was putting it in action.

The Way

The Bible has many verses on the importance of scholarship and wisdom: in fact, a particular book might come to your mind about this exact topic. Proverbs is a celebration of learning as it comes from the hand of a man blessed with God's wisdom to the eye of anyone desiring to find the knowledge of God, which chapter 2:1-4 says can be found if we turn our ears to wisdom, apply our hearts to understanding, call out for understanding, and search learning like a treasure. Learning brings safety from the wicked (2:12), blessings (3:13-14), power, and strength (24:5). But we cannot come by wisdom without a love of learning, without applying our hearts to instruction and our ears to the words of knowledge (23:12).

In 1 Chronicles 1:9-12, Solomon asks for knowledge above any other blessing from God; in turn, he is blessed by wealth and honor as well. In Psalm 119:66, David requests for God to teach him "knowledge and good judgment." And in Colossians 2:2-4, understanding is described as "full riches" while wisdom and knowledge are "treasures."

The Want

My request for my sons to have philologia is not simply my desire for them to have good grades or to get full-ride scholarships to Ivy League schools (though I wouldn't turn these away). I desire for my boys to find beauty in discovering the intricacies and anomalies of our world; I want them to be in awe of the extravagant and what we, as we grow old, too often find insignificant.

As I watch my oldest son grow, I love how he reminds me to slow down and *see*. My eyes may be open each day, but when am I actually *seeing*? But Jack sees so much, and he finds so much wonderful. His world is beautiful, and he doesn't tire of finding more beauty in it each day.

When he was first learning to jump, he barely got both feet off of the ground; now he *leaps*. The newness of learning and growing is still so new to him; that is a blessing I pray he does not outgrow.

Lord,

I see my children discovering their world—your world—every day. They show astonishment and delight in learning, and I pray you continue to foster that joy. I want them to desire to grow in true wisdom, in you, but also to find specific interests that bring them pleasure as they learn more about the different talents you have given them and the different blessings you have put in this world.

Philologia is a light we are all born with. Instead of letting this light grow dim, I pray it roars into a mighty flame. Let us, as parents, do what we can to fan this flame, and may the obvious excitement of our children for discovery be contagious. Let our whole family catch philologia and **never** recover.

We are so blessed.

Amen.

Peace

The Word

I must admit my disappointment with the definition of the word "Peace" online: "nonwarring...mutual harmony...freedom from civil commotion or violence." This definition is insufficient, to say the least. Though I hope their lives are free from violence and war, my expectation for my children in the manner of them having the blessing of peace is not limited to this meaning.

But what is someone to do if the internet fails to meet her research needs? Open a book. And since my dictionary is packed away, I remember having an old copy of a thesaurus around. What a treasure of a find. The inside cover reads with the inscription *To Aunt Bertha with love from Helen, Christmas 1933*, and many of the words have more than a mere listing of synonyms. In fact, George Crabb, compiler and writer, writes two columns on the word "peace" alone, first giving the similar words "quiet, calm, tranquility," then explaining, "*Peace* is derived through French from Latin *pax*" (549). In an effort to explore the true meaning of these terms, he goes on to compare and contrast the difference between each of these synonyms. Thankfully, his writing gives much more depth:

> » *Peace implies an exemption from public or private broils...*
> » *Every affectionate family will naturally act in such a manner as to promote peace among all its members...*
> » *A good man enjoys the peace of a good conscience...*
> » *People are...calm inasmuch as they are exempt from the commotion which at any given moment rages around them...*
> » *A house is designated as a peaceful abode as it is remote from the bustle and hurry of a multitude. (549)*

In 1933, Aunt Bertha received a beautiful gift from Helen. I wonder if it sat on the shelf of a peaceful home then. I wonder if it does now.

The Way

"Grace and peace to you...." And so begins Galatians, Ephesians, Philippians, Colossians, 1 and 2

Thessalonians, 1 and 2 Timothy, Titus, Philemon, 1 and 2 Peter, and Jude. *Peace* is obviously an important blessing the writers wish to grant to the readers of these letters.

God, who is not a God of disorder but of peace (1 Corinthians 14:33, Philippians 4:9, Hebrews 13:20, and 1 Thessalonians 5:23), promises peace to His people (Psalm 85:8)–a peace that is found in His very presence in our lives (2 Thessalonians 3:16). His Son is the Prince of Peace (Isaiah 9:6) who "Himself is our peace" and whose purpose was to preach peace "to you who were far away and...to those who were near" in life and to become the ultimate maker of peace in His death (Ephesians 2: 13-17).

We are called to live in peace (1 Corinthians 7:15 and 2 Corinthians 13:11) because "blessed are the peacemakers, for they will be called children of God" (Matthew 5:9).

The Want

Of course I want my children to be children of God. My hope for peace in the lives of my children is twofold. First, I pray they bring peace. I want others to think of my sons as soothers of situations, calmers of crowds, quieters of chaos. I also don't want violence to surround them, brought on by them or brought on to them.

But I want more, and I can—I am their mother.

I want our home to promote that peace and their homes, in the future, to continue the trend. I want my sons and my future daughter to have a calmness and peacefulness about them. I want them to be able to quiet the chaos of their own hearts and minds.

My second son, Jonas, displayed signs of peace even from the first days of his life. I have always been in awe of the beauty of his spirit. I'm not saying he doesn't ever get upset, but I feel a strength radiating off of him, and have from within our first moments together, that I can only describe as *peace*. Getting to know him has made me more aware of how dearly I pray for this quality to stay with him always, and to bless Jack and our future children as well.

Jonas's peace has also had a positive reaction on me; peace isn't really a part of my make-up, but I'm beginning to better understand what it is now that I have stared into its big brown eyes.

Lord,

I am not a naturally peaceful person. I plan, think, worry, wonder, wish, plan, second-guess, question, plan...to the point of franticness at times. But I've seen your peace—when I slow down long enough—in the grandeur and minuteness of your creation, in the slow smiles and thoughtful expressions of my children, and in the beauty of the moment when I quiet my spirit and enjoy *now*.

I pray my children can have peace despite the "commotion which at any given moment rages around them" or "the bustle and hurry of a multitude" (Crabb 549). Give them the certainty of your love, Christ's sacrifice, and the truth of heaven, and may that certainty be the strength to look at any day and any situation with a peace that "passes all understanding" (Philippians 4:7).

We are so blessed.

Amen.

Purity

The Word

"Always do right. This will gratify some people, and astonish the rest" (Mark Twain 436).

Purity is linked to the word "Virtuous:"

> From Low Latin *virtuosus*...indicated the proper character of man (*vir*), the sum of all manly virtues. It now signifies the person who is at heart morally *good*, who abstains from vice, acts in the spirit of the *moral* law, is brave, valorous, and strong in principles... *pure* in deed and thought, *upright*, honest... being *chaste*, *pure*, unspotted...[promoting] goodness, morality, purity, in the community. (Crabb 701)

Too often we connect the word *purity* to *prude*, but being pure doesn't mean you cannot have fun; it does mean that your ideals of what is fun promote "goodness, morality, purity" and show that you have the "proper character." I appreciate that the above definition aptly brings forth that purity requires *bravery*. In a world that too quickly accepts contamination as the norm, we are called to be clean. This is no easy task. After all, "few men have virtue to withstand the highest bidder" (George Washington 436). Morals shouldn't be sold out at the auction block. They shouldn't be dropped at will; true purity is persistent.

The Way

"Do not conform any longer to the pattern of this world" (Romans 12:2). Again, the *bravery* required of the pure is evident. So, the quality of courage is one I will discuss more fully later. Standing for something that is not along the same "pattern of the world" is a challenge. Also a challenge is keeping your mind only on whatever is true, noble, right, pure, lovely, admirable, excellent, and praiseworthy (Philippians 4:8). This list is to be an ever-present, decision-making guide.

We are a new people, and that requires us to "put off" our old selves and "put on the new self, created to be like God in true righteousness and holiness" (Ephesians 4:22-24). Keeping righteous and holy means we cannot even "give the devil a foothold" (Ephesians 4:27) in our lives, because he will use any manner he can to take us over. We were once in darkness, but now we are in the light of God (Ephesians 5:8), so we *know better* and should therefore *act better*. We have to use discernment to be "pure and blameless" until Christ comes again (Philippians 1:10–11).

And I haven't even gotten to the specific purity hot topic. Sex.

- » *"There must not be even a hint of sexual immorality, or any kind of impurity" (Ephesians 5:3).*
- » *Remember what your father has taught you about keeping away from the immoral woman; lusting after her will destroy you (Proverbs 6:2–33).*
- » *You should avoid sexual immorality and learn to control your body in a way that is holy (1 Thessalonians 4:3–5).*
- » *Run away from sexual immorality because "your body is a temple" (1 Corinthians 6:12–20).*
- » *If you don't have any self-control, you have as few defenses in life as a "city whose walls are broken down" (Proverbs 25:28).*

Our bodies are not to do what we please with: they are a temple, a vessel of worship to the One who Created us, and self-control (which requires self-evaluation, prayer, self-honesty, and accountability) is our best line of defense in a world that tells us to do whatever whenever however.

The Want

I honestly believe goodness is easier for (perhaps self-control is more available in) certain people. So, my first prayer is that goodness is easy for my children, that self-control is abundant, that "thinking on such things" listed in Philippians 4:8 comes fairly naturally.

Secondly, when virtue is a striving, may virtue win! Whatever bravery is required for my children to build the walls around their purity, to worship God with their bodies rather than embarrass Him, to be plaid when the "pattern of the world" is polka dot—I want that strength in them.

Lord,

You know our hearts. You know the hearts of my children, now and later. You know with what ease or with what strife they will work for purity. May it be ease. May goodness not be a difficulty, but a natural characteristic. Bless them with surroundings and with people who encourage righteous living, and with sense and strength to avoid anything and anyone who reassures an apathy or sympathy for corruption.

- Give them strong legs, to run from immorality.
- Give them strong backs, to build permanent walls of defense against the world's way.
- Give them strong necks, to turn their eyes away from things they don't need to see.
- Give them strong hands, to pull away from places they should not go.

- Give them strong tongues, to remain void of filth when filth is easy and obvious.
- Give them strong hearts, to beat always in truth, nobility, righteousness, purity, admirability, excellence, and praise-worthiness.

We are so blessed.

Amen.

Passion

The Word

Passion is a noun whose meaning connects to "strong love" and a "compelling emotion or feeling" with roots from Middle English, Old French, and Medieval Latin ("Passion"). This word is not calm, passive, or quiet, which is all the more reason to place it directly after my prayer for my children to have peace and purity, because I do believe one can have a properly directed passion (a pure passion, a peaceful passion, so to speak) even though "passion" is often linked with the word "lust." In fact, if you look up "Passionate" in *Crabb's English Synonymes*, you are immediately directed to the word "angry" (548) which gives the synonym "hasty" (59).

"Passion" gets a bad wrap. But even two of Crabb's descriptions of "Passionate" can be directed positively to show the elements of this word I want my children to exhibit:

> » *passionate expresses a habit of the mind...*

> *a passionate man is habitually prone to be passionate. (59)*

With a passion directed towards a "compelling emotion" of "strong love" for their spouses, my children can keep the "habit of the mind" to continually be "habitually prone to be passionate" in their loving, life-long marriage. This blessing will actually guide them away from lustful passions of a myriad of partners that the world says is acceptable, if they can direct their passionate ardor to one deserving person.

The Way

"Husbands, love your wives…love your wives as you love yourself…he who loves his wife loves himself" (Ephesians 5:25-28).

I've often reflected on God's call for women to be submissive and men to love their wives. In recent years, I've come to the conclusion that this call is for us to go beyond what is natural for us. I hate to use sweeping generalizations, but women tend to find it easy to lead, and men usually have little trouble in taking care of their desires. So God asks us, in our marriages, to do the opposite of what is easy for us—women: step back, and let your husband step up; men: put your wives' quiet desires ahead of yours, and cherish her openly and honestly. That cherishing makes a passionate marriage.

Genesis describes the union of marriage as two people being united into one (2:24), and this union is supposed to continue on in passion throughout growing old together: "May you rejoice in the wife of your youth...may you ever be captivated by her love" (Proverbs 5:18-19). Notice that Proverbs doesn't say, "May you endure your lives together." These verses ask for the blessing of a forever passion: captivated in love.

The Want

A lot of people don't know this about me, but I actually suffer from the illness known as "hopeless romantic syndrome." It's quite serious, and there is no known cure. Some people think being let down in romance is the best medicine to alleviate this syndrome, but true hopeless romantics still hold on to a constant desire for fulfillment.

My illness is the direct cause of this desire for my children to have passionate marriages, to live in captivation that doesn't diminish as they grow older but becomes stronger in practice and patience. The belly-butterflies won't be present every day, but they can return once in a while, as long as my sons (and son-in-law) remember to love their wives in the way they are charged in Ephesians, and as long as they understand that love cannot be just understood, it has to be stated-in multiple ways-often.

But that doesn't mean all the work and no payoff rests on the shoulders of the husbands. The cherished wife finds her call to submission less aggravating, and she is prone to be passionate in return. Besides, my true hope is that it isn't a large amount of extra work for my sons (and son-in-law) to openly treasure their wives. I want them to find women who deserve that affection. And I want my one-day daughter to be deserving.

Truly, I hope my hopeless romantic syndrome is hereditary, that it brings a level of romantic and passionate fulfillment (and not frustration) to the marriages of my children.

Lord,

You made us dynamic characters. We can be both peaceful and strong, pure and passionate. Passion can be directed to inappropriate channels, but it can also be beautiful when it is used in the way of your Word. Please let my children hold their passion in waiting for the person who deserves it, and then let that passion overwhelm (in a good way) those young couples as they grow into old couples.

I want my children to feel captivated in love, to cherish their spouses...and to be cherished always. Bless their marriages with a longevity that does not feel like imprisonment, but that is impassioned with the never-failing qualities set up in 1 Corinthians 13: patience, kindness, trust, humility, honor, selflessness, calmness, forgiveness, goodness, protection, hope, and endurance.

We are so blessed.

Amen.

Purpose

The Word

Although I may not agree with all of his philosophical ideals, I do appreciate Jose Ortega y Gasset's comment on the importance of having a life purpose: "Really to live is to be directed towards something, to progress towards a goal" (348). Purpose is "a point on which the soul may fix its intellectual eye" (Mary Shelley 348). The word means you have set your mind on "an object of pursuit" (Crabb 252). You cannot have purpose without these words: "steady," "serious resolution," and "resolute temper" (Crabb 252).

We are designed for specific tasks, the ultimate being to worship God with the talents He has blessed us with. This goal aligns with the dictionary definition: purpose is "the reason for which something exists or is done, made, or used" ("Purpose"). Our main reason of existence is to glorify, and we can do so by doing, making, and using ourselves with purpose for this purpose.

The Way

"We are all God's workmanship, created in Christ Jesus to do good works, which God prepared in advance for us to do" (Ephesians 2:10). These words can seem a heavy burden, trying to figure out what God wants us to do with our lives—but I prefer to see it as uplifting: God has known my life's purposes before I had life. He blessed us each with specific gifts, and we need to "live a life worthy of the calling" He has set up for us (Ephesians 4:1). This is a daily call, because we must make sure we are always "making the most of every opportunity" (Ephesians 5:15).

The first step is that we must, in everything we do, "acknowledge Him" (Proverbs 3:6). His name will be glorified in our lives if we allow Him to use His power to "fulfill every good purpose" He has for us (2 Thessalonians 1:11-12).

As we set goals in our life, as we try to find ways to use our talents to give our lives direction, we should *RUN* to fulfill our purpose; it is a prize we must keep in mind (1 Corinthians 9:24-27). In God's service, we each have a task to fulfill, and we will be rewarded (1 Corinthians 3:8-9). This reward is not only heaven, but a satisfying life as well.

God told Moses to rescue His people from Pharaoh: "I have raised you up for this very purpose, that my name might be proclaimed in all the earth" (Exodus 9:16, Romans 9:17). Moses didn't think this purpose suited him: "I am slow of speech and slow of tongue" (Exodus 4:10). Why would he second-guess his Creator? Sometimes our skills are obvious; sometimes they are quiet; sometimes they are easy to share; sometimes they are easy to hide...and sometimes God says, "I don't care what you think you are good at—you need to do this and trust that, if I give you a path and a purpose, I will give you a map and a means."

The Want

I grew up in a family who valued *purpose*. Your career, your relationships, your chores: find your purpose, search for your "bliss" (as my father likes to quote Joseph Campbell), and live a fulfilled life as you make and reach goals.

I pray my children see their talents clearly and feel they have a specific purpose in life. No...specific purpose**s**. These goals can change as they grow, but I want them to always know their life has direction and value. I love what I do: including my professor profession, motherhood, and other areas of my life that fulfill me and, I hope, that I do in such a way that God is glorified. My life is always an example to my kids, and I want to show them how to develop their talents and use these gifts to make their lives more meaningful.

Lord,

I can already see glimpses of the men my boys will be. Jack is a dynamic, quixotic sort–ready to laugh, learn, and love. Jonas is peaceful and pleasant, yet also strong and stubborn–with a thoughtful expression and a quiet cleverness. (Reader, take a moment to reflect on and give thanks for all the strengths of your child or children.)

Every strength we have can be weakness, every weakness a strength, depending on how much we let you intervene. Moses thought he wasn't eloquent enough to talk a powerful ruler into releasing your people, but you knew–through you–that anyone can accomplish the purpose set before him. Continue to give my children strengths, help them work out their weaknesses, and develop their trust in your guidance.

Show them ways to praise you with their talents; let your goodness be evident in their actions and accomplishments. And, I boldly ask, may they find a fulfilling and meaningful life as they always reach for greatness (that is not of them alone, but because of you). Great is your love; great is our purpose in you.

We are so blessed.

Amen.

Prosperity

The Word

I'd say most people would love to have "a successful, flourishing, or thriving condition, especially in financial respect" and "good fortune" ("Prosperity"). I've had money; I've had government-declared poverty. The prosperous times are easier and more satisfying; the poverty times made me realize that.

Prosperity isn't just affluence; it "includes likewise all that can add to the enjoyments of man" (Crabb 709).

Edmund Burke says, "It is, generally, in the season of prosperity that men discover their real temper, principles, and designs." Prosperity seems to be the gift that keeps on giving.

The Way

A highly misquoted verse warns that "the love of money is the root of all evil" (1 Timothy 6:10). Calvin Coolidge echoed this caution: "Prosperity is only an instrument to be used, not a deity to be worshipped."

With this advice in mind, we must remember that *prosperity* does not have to come with the idolization of wealth. The Bible does not condemn good fortune, as long as we honor God with our "first fruits" (an action that will even increase our success) (Proverbs 3:9-10). Obedience promises prosperity (Deuteronomy 5:33). And meek people (a word far from the vision of an Ebenezer Scrooge-like mindset) are promised peace and prosperity, as are those who work hard, respect God (Psalms 37:11), are generous (Proverbs 11:25), listen to instruction (16:20), trust God (28:25), and pursue righteousness (21:21).

In other words, prosperity is not a curse to devastation, but a blessing for those living their lives God-intended.

Give, and you will get.

Obey, and you will have abundance.

Heed, and you will achieve.

Live well, and you will live well.

The Want

My wish is for real riches to abound in the souls, and in the lives, of my children. And, honestly, I hope for them never to be in want (though, as I will discuss later with *compassion*, I hope they always look out for those who are). And I, as their mother, want all the best for them: I see no wickedness in praying for them to prosper.

Edmund Burke, as previously quoted, thinks prosperity is the perfect time for a man to truly learn whom he is. I can understand this, but with the perspective of one who has lived a few years at the mercy of prayer, hand-me-downs, and the kindness of those more fiscally fortunate. Having been in such a financial crunch as a teenager (when "having" seems to be everything), I now feel overwhelmed by our prosperity.

After we married, Jay and I didn't take out school loans. This was achieved by the generosity of my father paying for my undergraduate degree and our hard work as we took turns putting each other through graduate school. We were busy, we were tired, we were (at times) poor. But now, except for school loans from the first two and a half years for Jay and our mortgage, we are debt free.
Two incomes feel too good to be true.

So there can be times where money is tight—but I hope it's as they are wisely pursuing success, doing what needs to be done to fulfill their life's purpose. These are goals worth the short-term investment of temporarily tight wallets.

Lord,

I pray my children strive for success, thrive in lives abundant of good fortune. Let them not feel failure, but see mistakes as avenues for advance. If they have to give up wealth for a time, may it be for the progress of well-being.

In their prosperity, may they always acknowledge others–and **always** acknowledge you for every one of life's blessings. Your Word says prosperity can come to those who are obedient, meek, hardworking, generous–to those who respect, heed, trust, and pursue you. Since these are all qualities I have requested throughout this writing, I ask that you give them this nature, and then reward their life-diligence with the "real riches" that go along with the many layers of prosperity.

Bless them, keep them, and let them **flourish**!

We **are** so blessed.

Amen.

Perseverance

The Word

"A dream doesn't become reality through magic; it takes sweat, determination, and hard work" (Colin Powell).

Perseverance is "strict and steady...determination" (Crabb 207), "continued steady belief or efforts, withstanding discouragement or difficulty" ("Perseverance"). Hard workers continue even when the work gets harder.

"There is real virtue in the act of *perseverance*, without which many of our best intentions would remain unfulfilled and our best plans would be defeated" (Crabb 207). "There is always wisdom in *perseverance*" even if we seemingly fail (208). "Failure after long perseverance is much grander than never to have a striving good enough to be called a failure" (George Eliot).

Hard work is hard work, but there is righteousness in resolve.

The Way

"All hard work brings a profit, but mere talk leads only to poverty" (Proverbs 14:22-24). Here, the Proverbs reflect the common adage "easier said than done," but with the twist of "more blessed done than said." The Bible acknowledges that being a Christian, in and of itself, is hard work, but those who put in the effort are honored: "Now we ask you, brothers and sisters, to acknowledge those who **work hard** among you, who care for you in the Lord and who admonish you" (1 Thessalonians 5:12). Perseverance builds character, character builds hope, and "hope doesn't put us to shame" (Romans 5:3-5).

"Make every effort to add to your faith goodness; and to goodness, knowledge; and to knowledge, self-control; and to self-control, perseverance; and to perseverance, godliness; and to godliness, mutual affection; and to mutual affection, love" (2 Peter 1:5-7). Though this verse puts it in the middle of the list, perseverance is needed throughout the process of achieving and keeping all of these qualities: goodness, knowledge, self-control, perseverance, godliness, mutual affection, love. (Yes, even perseverance requires perseverance.)

"Let us throw off everything that hinders and the sin that so easily entangles. And let us run with perseverance the race marked out for us, fixing our eyes on Jesus, the pioneer and perfecter of faith" (Hebrews 12:1-2). This "race" refers overall to our life journeys and specifically to the different purposes that direct us in life. As someone who thinks running should be legally banned because of its intense degree of difficulty, I can completely connect to the wording of "run" being linked directly to "with perseverance." For me, there is no other way to run. But if I have a fixed mark, such as a weight loss goal or the reward of cookies and milk, running isn't any easier, but it is worth it. What is more worth it than the goal of Jesus?

The Want

I'm not saying life is always hard, but I'm also not saying it's always easy. The previous chapter spoke about having a purpose, achieving goals. As I wrote it, I added *perseverance* to my list of things I pray for my children. I hadn't thought of it before, but then it dawned on me: you can't thrive unless you strive.

Right now I have only two boys (with a daughter on the way). As a woman, I know that "hardworking" is at the top of many other women's qualifications for a husband. (Men want a hardworking wife as well, but they don't always think to ask for it in that specific way.) I want my sons to know the value of a dollar, to earn instead of owe, and to have a willingness to put in the time and effort required to make their families safe and sound, their spouses feel adored and taken care of, and their dreams reality.

My two-year-old is stubborn. I've recently started praying carefully about this quality; I dare not pray it away–but I am praying it towards a purpose. When I look up "stubborn" in my synonym file on Microsoft Word, what do I find? *Persevering*. Certain times in life we need to be stubborn. I want him to learn how to use this quality for good, not for annoyance...and never for evil.

My husband's company motto is "whatever it takes, and then some." We've joked about it every now and then, but sometimes life asks for "and then some." I want my kids to be ready, willing, and able to cope with those times.

Lord,

Your Proverbs explain the disasters that come with laziness (12:24, 19:15). Our society is sullied by the temptation of ease, but greatness doesn't come easily—and you know I want the best for my children, so gift them with the strength and sense to work hard. Grant them often the rewards of their diligence, and let them see the direct link between persistence and pleasure.

"Excellence is to do a common thing [living] in an uncommon way [in You]" (Booker T. Washington). When you say your burden is easy and your yoke light (Matthew 11:30), I don't think you mean that life won't have its challenges; you mean you'll be there with us all the way: you'll be our "rest" when we are "weary and burdened" (Matthew 11:28). Give my children the ability to face difficult situations, the might to carry on, and the wisdom to turn to you for comfort. Let others see your power through the powerful accomplishments they diligently achieve.

We are so blessed.

Amen.

Companionship

The Word

Ralph Waldo Emerson writes, "A friend may well be reckoned the masterpiece of Nature" (159).

Companionship is linked with "fellowship, camaraderie, togetherness" ("Companionship"). Being together, talking together–"it redoubleth joys, and cutteth griefs in half" (Francis Bacon 158) to have someone to share with. Indeed, "A *companion* takes part with us in some concern, and shares with us in the pleasure or the pain" (Crabb 81).

In *Don Quixote de la Mancha*, author Miguel de Cervantes writes, "Tell me what company you keep, and I'll tell you what you are" (66). And poet W.B Yeats says, "Think where man's glory most begins and ends, and say my glory was I had such friends" (159). "Such friends." Yeats and de Cervantes have pointed out a critical truth: the companions we keep will either help or hinder us in our Christian walk.

The Way

"A faithful friend is the medicine of life" (Ecclesiastes 6:16), but a bitter, addictive, and damaging drug it can be if we do not choose our friends wisely. Of course we must minister to people who need and do not know Jesus (Matthew 28:19's great commission), but we cannot "walk in the counsel of the wicked or stand in the way of the sinners or sit in the seat of mockers" (Psalm 1:1) and expect to keep all of the qualities listed in this book. Proverbs 12:26 tells us that righteous people are careful when picking friends; one who has unreliable friends will be ruined (Proverbs 18:24).

Good friends always love us (Proverbs 17:17) and give us "heartfelt advice" (27:9). They do not take lightly the task of friendship. Yes, friendship is a task. The old saying goes that you cannot have a friend without being a friend.

The Want

Making friends isn't exactly easy for me. I am generally reserved around new people, and I figure this causes some to feel that the effort in getting to know me might not be worth it, or, perhaps, that what they see is all I am. At this moment in my life, as I live and type, I am slightly overwhelmed by my blessings of companionship. And because of my reserve, I know these friends were directly put in my path—no, *shoved* at me, for only a great Force could bind such quick and necessary friendships in my life. I keep wondering why I am so blessed. Thankfully, my friends find my being in their lives a blessing as well.

My husband Jay and I both recognize the times in our lives when being good was made easier because of good friends. Earlier when I prayed for purity to be easy for my children, I knew I had to add *companionship* to my list of requests, because it is more difficult to have the first without the second.

Lord,

Echoing in my ears, I can hear Jack's sweet listing off in his prayers before I lay him down for naptime only an hour ago: "Thank you [for] Jack, Thank you Jonas, Thank you Mama, Thank you Daddy, Thank you good friends...." And at least twice a day we mention our thankfulness to you for the companions you have blessed us with. What a beautiful gift is the company of like-minded Christians. (In Jack's case, this means friends who also love the playground and clay; in our case, it is someone to talk with, hope with, pray with, commiserate with, cheer with....)

"Thank you good friend." I want to repeat that appreciation, because I too often ask without praising.

But I do have to ask—let this blessing continue. Give us, as parents, good friends who will help us in our marriage, our walk with you, and our great challenge of parenthood. And give our children good friends who will help them be good, learn grace, keep going, love God, share gain, develop gifts, play games, know gladness, and achieve greatness.

And may my children always, always recognize the gift and praise you: "Thank you good friends."

We are so blessed.

Amen.

Compassion

The Word

"With great power comes great responsibility" (*Spiderman*). Uncle Ben's warning to Peter Parker is something we should consider as well. With all the blessings I am praying my children receive, I want to make sure they never forget to help others: to show compassion. "Only when the sense of the pain of others begins–does man begin" (Yevgeny Yevtushenko 406).

Compassion is an acknowledgement for the suffering of others accompanied with the wish to alleviate it ("Compassion"). With a similar meaning, *benevolence* "is an affair of the heart…the wish or intention to do good…wherever there is an opportunity of doing good" (Crabb 116). Mason Cooley explains the effects of compassion, not just on those that are aided, but also on the one offering the aid: "Compassion brings us to a stop, and for a moment we rise above ourselves."

The Way

We are called to "look not only to [our] own interests, but also to the interests of others" (Philippians 2:4). Doing so will make us "rise above ourselves," as Cooley said; indeed "a kind man benefits himself" (Proverbs 11:17), and "a generous man will prosper; he who refreshes others will himself be refreshed" (11:25). God blesses us when we are kind to those in need (14:21; 22:9). We are to be clothed in "compassion, kindness, humility, gentleness, and patience" (Colossians 3:12), to "love one another, be compassionate and humble" (1 Peter 3:8). Second Corinthians 8:7 explains that even the most well-rounded, gifted, or hard-working individual is not complete without compassion: "Since you excel in everything... see that you also excel in this grace of giving."

Sometimes the attributes we want to exhibit in life are easier to incorporate into our daily existence when we have an example; when it comes to compassion, we have the greatest Example of all. The Psalmist praises God for His benevolence (Psalms 86:15; 103:8). The compassionate Christ healed the blind (Matthew 20:24), fed the hungry (Mark 8:2), and taught the ignorant (Mark 6:34). His kindness was the ultimate—He took care of those who didn't even recognize a need, those living in sin and defiance. Just as the father gladly accepted back his prodigal son (Luke 15:20), when people deserved the worst, God showed tenderness (Lamentations 3:32; Jonah 4:1).

When we deserve the worst, God shows us tenderness: "For God so loved the world, that He gave His only Son" (John 3:16).

The Want

My initial intention when I wrote down the word *compassion* in my outline for this writing changed direction as I started my research. I hope my children are generous, loving, helpful, and kind—but now I see those traits encompass even more than tithing on Sunday or supporting a Christian organization (though these are noble and necessary as well). Compassion can range from funds to friendliness. A much-needed smile or "hello," a donation to an African Christian hospital, a pause in your frantic house cleaning or cooking to kneel on the level of a child and *listen*: all of these actions are, hopefully, spurred on by compassion. (Another cause could be guilt, and I hope my children are able to give with a generous-heart and not a guilt-ridden one.)

As I grew up, my parents had me tithe

even my small allowance. They weren't trying to force generosity, but rather to encourage the early habit of compassion. Fifty cents in the plate every month wasn't going to change the world, but it did change how I looked at money: it, as with every gift of God, is meant to praise God.

I pray for my children to be prosperous, to know success and comfort; in their comfort, may they not ignore those in distress. Having compassion will make them better friends, spouses, parents, citizens, humans, and Christians.

Here is small math analogy inspired by the transitive property (my favorite formula):

> If love = God (1 John 4:8) and God is compassionate (Isaiah 54:10; Lamentations 3:22), then love is compassionate. And if love never fails (1 Corinthians 13:8), then likewise our compassion for others shouldn't either.

Lord,

Some people are more inherently compassionate; I'm not sure if that is a trait we're biologically passed down or not, so I know that means I have to live as an example. Sometimes I feel overwhelmed by all the good that needs to be done. I don't want a sense of dread or impossibility to keep my children from helping others. Let their eyes be opened to the ways they can reach out. Make obvious how they can use their skills and talents to serve you in benevolence to others. Let them not be tempted by complacency; let them not give to be seen giving.

True compassion was shown in your rescuing people who didn't truly deserve to be rescued. I think that our family members are often the ones we least desire to show sympathy. When you live with someone, cruelty is easier than consideration, meanness than mercy, tyranny than tenderness. But "charity starts at home," so the saying goes. So I ask that you focus the hearts of my children to beginning their ministry of clemency with their family—me, their father, their siblings, and later their spouses and children—and then let it expand to encompass all areas of their lives.

We are so blessed—show us how to live the blessing.

Amen.

Courage

The Word

According to Robert Louis Stevenson, courage is "the footstool of the Virtues, upon which they stand" (77). True. Without courage we cannot remain always pure or peaceful, we cannot follow our purpose or gain prosperity, and we cannot persevere. "*Courage* is the power of the mind which bears up against the evil that is in prospect...we require *courage* to bear down all the obstacles which oppose themselves to us" (Crabb 219).

Bravery is not a lack of fear, but a recognition of and opposition to it: "Courage is resistance to fear, mastery of fear-not absence of fear" (Mark Twain 78). We can be brave by nature, or valor can come when we most need it. Ernest Hemingway calls having "guts...grace under pressure," and Shakespeare writes that "courage mounteth with occasion" (77). A courageous person isn't foolhardy, but is ready to take on a challenge. If we can "screw [our] courage to the sticking-place...we'll not fail" (Shakespeare 77).

The Way

"Be strong and courageous" (Deuteronomy 31:6, 31:7, 31:23; Joshua 1:6, 1:7, 1:9, 1:18, 10:25; 1 Chronicles 28:20; 2 Chronicles 32:7). I think that was the longest in-text citation I have ever typed. God must be serious about courage. We are told to be on guard, "be courageous, be strong" (1 Corinthians 16:13), "stand firm" (Ephesians 6:14), and to "rise up" when a particular matter is up to us to deal with–to "take courage and do it" (Ezra 10:4).

But how, God? How can we give our all in a world that tells us to give in?

- » "Be strong *in the Lord* and in His mighty power. Put on the full armor of God so that you can take your stand against the devil's schemes" (Ephesians 6:10-11).
- » "The Lord will be your confidence and will keep your foot from being snared" (Proverbs 3:36).
- » "I can do everything through Him who gives me strength" (Philippians 4:13).

And the end of Deuteronomy 31:6 and Joshua 1:9 explain that we are able to "be strong and courageous" because God is with us!

The Want

Since many of the other qualities I want for my children won't hold up in the line of fire without courage, this trait is a must-pray-for item. Of course, often I ask for things to be easy for my children, but, in the times they are not, I request boldness.

One of the reasons I so value valor is because I believe the need can bring us to our knees. The verses on the previous page show that strength comes *"through Him."* So, when we need to be strong, we must come to Him. There is no might without the Master; there is no confidence without Christ.

Lord,

Bless my babies with boldness. When they are afraid, may they trust in you (Psalms 56:3). May they not be afraid of bad things, because they know you are with them always (Psalm 23:4). And let the comfort of your protection give them the power to conquer anything.

Strong hearts are not hard hearts—they are focused on and conscious of you. Direct my children to you, and when the path in front of them is rough, let them know the worth of the way: let them continue in confident courage to your throne. One day you will hold us and say, "Well done, good and faithful child of mine" (Matthew 25:23). I pray the desire for this acknowledgement gives muscle to the faith and actions of my sweet children always.

We are so blessed.

Amen.

Cleverness

The Word

To be clever is to have "sharp or quick intelligence... inventiveness or originality" ("Clever"), to "act expeditiously and efficiently with mind and body" (Crabb 397). A similar word is *gumption* (far too unused in this day and age): someone with gumption has "a quickness of perception, the possession of much common sense;" his mind is sharp, keen, and acute (Crabb 397).

"It is not enough to have a good mind. The main thing is to use it well" (Rene Descartes 223). Cleverness is intelligence in action.

The Way

Proverbs 23:4 exposes a warning: we shouldn't put all of our efforts into trying to get rich, and we shouldn't trust only in our own cleverness. Wisdom, intelligence, knowledge—these were the first temptation: to be like God, to know like God (Genesis 3:6). But this doesn't mean being clever is a sin; it means we must have God as our intellectual foundation, to trust in Him and not only in our own resourcefulness. This blessing of brainpower can be a curse if we don't use it appropriately.

Wisdom and skill (the combination of the two being cleverness) are gifts God gives for His purpose in Exodus 28:3, Exodus 31:3, and Exodus 35:31–and the gift God can give us to work His will in our own purpose.

The Want

When I was going to graduate school for my master's in education, I remember hearing professors say we shouldn't use words like *you are so smart*. Instead, we should be specific in our praise: *you solved the problem*. But, honestly, I want my kids to be *so smart*. And, again, I'm their mom, so I can want the world for them.

But I don't just want book smarts or math smarts or test smarts–I want *cleverness*. I worry cleverness has been too often linked with *craftiness or cunning*; all three can have a bad connotation. But in my review of cleverness, it is the mixing of the best of smarts, practicality, and application. You know something, you know how it applies, and you know how to apply it.

Lord,

Cleverness is not over-confidence, but well-placed confidence in the wisdoms and skills you've given, acknowledgement of limitations, and the desire to overcome weaknesses in order to become a more well-rounded servant of the Master.

Please grant my children the cleverness to navigate the challenges of life, to know that in and through you and your wisdom, they can learn, grow, gain—and then share their wisdom and its resulting blessings to others. In school, in relationships, in work: may the tasks before them appear doable because they know you've given them the resources to figure things out. (And sometimes the best of those resources, the clever person knows, is asking another—or asking The Other.)

We are so blessed.

And we know it.

Amen

Health

The Word

Juvenal says, "You should pray for a sound mind in a sound body" (188). These blessings, according to John Locke, are the first step towards happiness: "A sound mind in a sound body, is a short but full description of a happy state in this world. He that has these two, has little more to wish for" (188).

When we first think of health, we think of "freedom from disease or ailment," though the word also encompasses "soundness of body or mind" ("Health"). My wellness-professor father would change that *or* to *and*.

"Life is not merely being alive, but being well" (Martial 188). Because I want a full and fulfilling life for my children, I pray for their health.

The Way

Health is more than a fit body. Third John 1:2 says, "Dear friend, I pray that you may enjoy good health and that all may go well with you even as your soul is getting along well." The prayer here is for *all* to go well—for even the *soul* to be well.

In some cases, Proverbs promises wellbeing as the reward for proper living. Proverbs 3:7-8 in particular says that a healthy respect of God will give us a healthy life. David, the man after God's own heart, is described in 1 Samuel 16:12 and 17:42 as "glowing with health." This phrasing makes me feel that more than physical fitness is being mentioned here. David's health was holistic—his body, mind, and spirit were working in harmony and happiness.

When David is in need of help from Nabel, he sends over a message: "Long life to you! Good health to you and your household. Good health to all that is yours!" (1 Samuel 25:6). Ironically enough, when Nabel acts in the manner of his name (which means "fool" according to 1 Samuel 25:25) and ignores David's blessings and request, Nabel's health fails him, and he dies (1 Samuel 25:37). Nabel is not concerned over his own wellbeing: he is gluttonous with food and wine (1 Samuel 25:36) and foolish in his decision-making (1 Samuel 25:25). He doesn't treat his body (or his mind) like a temple of God (1 Corinthians 6:19). His lack of respect for others and for himself brings his ruin.

The Want

Jack has always had issues with his health. He spent the first months of his life battling colic; he spent his first Christmas Eve in the children's ER with pneumonia at only three and a half months old; and then he got eczema so bad that his skin was raw. A year later he was in the ER again, dehydrated with pneumonia. At age two we took him to an allergist who explained, "Jack is allergic to life."

Holding him as he coughs, sometimes struggling to get a breath in, I remember how careful I was with my diet when I was pregnant, and how much I prayed for a healthy baby.

But it could be so much worse, I remind myself. And I continue my prayers for Jack's health. His dad had similar problems and grew out of them, for the most part. Jack can too. It's sad to hear him wheeze and to know that a fun day at the park could make for a bad night of coughing, but we continue to let him be a little boy–with our eyes on him a little more cautiously than we would otherwise.

On the other hand, Jonas is six months old and experiencing his first cold. I cannot help praising the Lord for the health of this child. We were still trying to get Jack's eczema in check at this time in his life, and Jonas has a stuffy nose and a cough but is still, for the most part, sleeping through the night. And I pray his good health continues.

Also, I know my treatment of my own body, mind, and spirit will be an example to my children. I am a temple of God—my work towards my wellness will reflect what I think about the Creator's creations, specifically His creating me. I want to be a good example, and I want to harvest a respect for self-care that will glean a healthier life.

Lord,

The sweet boys I have now, and the sweet children to come—may they have good health. I want them to have lives filled with adventures that won't be restricted by allergies or a poor disposition. May their minds, bodies, and spirits work in harmony—in you—to give them lives that are more than mere motion. Let them be enriched, thrilled, and vibrant: let them be "glowing with health." Let others see the beauty that this harmony of being brings, and make them want to know where it comes from. It comes from you!

I know life will have its challenges, and in my boldness as a mother who loves her children with all, I pray to you that serious health issues are not one of those challenges. Give them energy and stamina to carry out your message of love, to grow into the destiny you have prepared for them. And give them a respect for their bodies, minds, and spirits that leads them towards an appropriate treatment of themselves: let them not ignore the elements of healthy living, but to incorporate daily the choices that will make them holistically richer.

My dad often signs his letters "In Wellness"—and it is "in wellness" that I want my children to sign their **Letter of Life**. May they love, laugh, and live in a well-being they know is a gift from you. And may they do their parts to honor their temple-bodies in thanks for the wellness you give them.

We are so blessed.

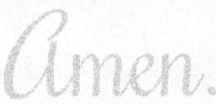

Humor

The Word

"Humor is emotional chaos remembered in tranquility" (James Thurber 208). Indeed, we often say, "Some day we'll look back on this and laugh." A sense of humor can get people through awkward or tough situations. Romain Gary goes as far as to say that "humor is an affirmation of dignity, a declaration of man's superiority to all that befalls him" (206). It's harder to conquer someone who knows how to laugh.

Defined, humor is "the sense of wit" (Crabb 425), the ability "of perceiving what is amusing or comical," or the knack for "expressing the amusing or comical" ("Humor").

The Way

Honestly, this characteristic gave me the hardest time as I researched its Biblical connection. Laughing doesn't always get the best wrap in the Bible. Sarah laughed at God's promise for her to have children in her old age (Genesis 18:12), and Mr. Wisdom himself, King Solomon, says that "laughter is madness" (Ecclesiastes 2:2).

And yet, read all of Ecclesiastes. He also says that hard work (Ecclesiastes 2:17) and wisdom (which he devoted the entire book of Proverbs praising) are meaningless (Ecclesiastes 2:15). This was a time when King Solomon's heart was in despair (Ecclesiastes 2:20). It's hard to have a good laugh when you feel heavy with the idea that all "is meaningless, a chasing after the wind" (Ecclesiastes 2:26).

But God doesn't want us to despair.

Psalm 98:4, 100:1-2, 66:1-3, 81:1, 95:1, 98:4, and 100:1-3 all encourage us to make a "joyful noise unto God." "Make a *loud* noise, and rejoice, and sing praise!" (Psalm 98:4).

Generally this "noise" is connected to singing, but notice the latter verse says *and sing*. What if the joyful noise unto the Lord is *laughter*?

The Want

I didn't mean to rock theology with that statement, but I do think God delights in our delight— the sound of our healthy laughter (at appropriate things, of course), is a song. It is a sign of trust. *Things will be okay. Life is good. God is good.*

On a list of desired characteristics in the perfect mate, a good sense of humor usually makes the top ten. Of course everyone's "sense" is different, and what we really want is a "well-aligning" sense of humor.

The first thing that attracted me to my husband Jay was his wit. We got to know each other through instant messenger (like texts over the computer in the days before we all had cell phones) and emails. He made me laugh, and he brought out my natural wit in return. Even today, when I see something subtly funny, I think, *I wish Jay were here. He'd get it.*

I say Jonas is either smiling or scowling (his thinking face, perhaps). Jack loves to laugh. We are already seeing their senses of humor blossom, and it's funny to have little jokes with them.

Early on in our dating, I told Jay I always wanted there to be music in my future home. Now a mom, I admit that I delight in silence, but only as a break from the sounds of delight from my boys. When it isn't a guitar, piano, or someone singing...the music I want always rippling through my home is the laughter of those I love.

Lord,

Your creation is dynamic. We hurt: we heal. We laugh: we cry. And though tears are a healthy release, I pray my children's lives are fuller of the sound of their own laughter than that of crying.

Wit is obviously an important element of life to me, for me to list it along with courage and perseverance. I guess I've noticed that endurance is often easier if we are able to laugh through life.

Don't let my children laugh to hurt-you or others. Let their laughter be a healing for themselves, for their friends, and for their families. May it be a sign of your goodness, of their acknowledgement and appreciation of that goodness. May they find life beautiful, and funny. If laughter is the best medicine, give my family an extreme dose.

We are so blessed.

Amen.

 Happiness

The Word

America was founded, declared independent, in part with the "unalienable rights" for man of "the pursuit of happiness" ("The Declaration of Independence"). In this country, happiness is a major life goal. Happiness relates to "pleasurable sensations" and is "a compound of body and soul;" though it is "sought for by various means and with great eagerness," it "often lies much more within our reach than we are apt to imagine" (Crabb 399). "No man is happy who does not think himself so" (Pubilius Syrus 184). Indeed, happiness is a state of mind.

Often it is thought of as shallow, as fleeting-but happiness is only thus when shallow or fleeting desires are met. True happiness is deep. Crabb explains it well:

> Happiness is not to be found in the possession of great wealth, of great power, of great dominions, of great splendor, or the unbounded indulgences of any one appetite or desire; but in moderate possessions

with a heart tempered by religion and virtue for the enjoyment of that which God has bestowed upon us. (399)

The Way

God does tell us we, as Christians, will suffer in life (Romans 8:17), but that doesn't mean He wants life to be a suffering. He calls us to be joyful always–linking that joy with prayer and giving thanks (1 Thessalonians 5:16–18). Perhaps this verse shows us that one of the keys to happiness is being grateful. Ecclesiastes 2:26 also shares a key to gaining this blessing: if we please God, He will bless us with "wisdom, knowledge, and happiness."

The Psalms are filled with every emotion–and the great joy that can be our gift from a gracious God is one of them.

- » "You make me glad by your deeds, O Lord; I sing for joy at the works of your hands" (Psalm 92:4).
- » "Let us sing for joy" (Psalm 95:1).
- » "Let all who take refuge in you be glad" (Psalm 4:11).

> "I will be glad and rejoice in you" (Psalm 9:2).

Again and again it is made clear—happiness, the non-fleeting kind, is rooted in the Lord, and we are to praise Him for the blessings of life that make us glad.

The Want

Sometimes a delicious pizza makes me happy, but if that was where I built the foundation of my life-happiness, I'd be pretty miserable as I glared at the last dustings of crumbs on the pan. The temptation with happiness is to let the miniscule, the unimportant, rule our fuel for joy. The small niceties in life can be enjoyed, but our faith, and therefore our happiness, must have much more solidity and depth.

I want my children to have *all levels* of happiness—the shallow delight in pizza and the fullness of gladness in the works of His hands. I want my children to know the beauty of the little things, and the overwhelming grandeur of God.

I'm so thankful I found Crabb's wording: "moderate possessions with a heart tempered by religion and virtue" (399). When God is the foundation of our happiness, the entire structure will rise in joy.

Lord,

I feel things strongly: ups are high up, and lows are down low. Because my moods waver, I understand the value of true happiness in you. And I want that for my children. I want them to be in awe, to enjoy, to know gladness in what they have and in the journey of reaching goals. Let my children know, ultimately, that you are the Father of Blessings—that their happiness not only springs life from you, but is you.

In the joys that you bring them, give them hearts and lips that say, "This is because of you! Thank you! Thank you!" I've learned in my study of this word that happiness and thankfulness aren't loosely linked—they are bound to each other. Grant my children happy, grateful hearts.

We are so blessed. (Thank you! Thank you!)

Amen.

The Word

"Hope! Of all ills that men endure, the only cheap and universal cure" (Abraham Cowley 201). And the reason it can cure ills is because hope is "the feeling that what is wanted can be had or that events will turn out for the best" ("Hope"). And to hope is to "look forward to with desire and reasonable confidence" ("Hope").

The last word of that definition is imperative, and Crabb also links the word hope with the word *confidence* (421-22). Hope isn't a whim. It isn't idle. Hope is active assurance.

The Way

When we have hope in the Lord, we will not be put to shame (Psalm 25:3). If we keep our confidence in Him, follow His ways, we will be exalted (Psalm 37:34). During times when it feels there is nothing worth searching for, worth waiting for, we can have a firm hope in God (Psalm 39:7).

As our souls feel "downcast" and "disturbed," we are told to put our hope in the Lord and to praise Him (Psalm 42:5, 11; 43:5). The Psalmist had times of triumph and despair, and his words, paraphrased above, show just some of the repetition of his foundation of *active assurance* of God and in God. David's life and songs are an expression of his knowledge that God's delivered us in the past and will deliver us over and over again (2 Corinthians 1:10).

Without Christ, there is no hope (Ephesians 2:12), but because of Him, we have "faith and love that spring from the hope stored up" for us in heaven (Colossians 1:5). The resurrection is the reason for our resolve.

The Want

As I was lying next to Jack in his bed tonight, a wave of anxiety swept over me. I don't know if I showed it on my face, but Jack's sweet voice asked me, "Mama, you okay?" He's only a two-and-a-half year-old boy. How could he be so intuitive? I didn't know what to say at first, but I decided such a well-sensing question deserved an honest answer.

"I'm worried, Jack."

"Don't be sad, Mama. Don't cry." Jack touched my eyes, which were dry until his sweetness overwhelmed me, taking the place of my anxiousness. "Be happy," he encouraged me, smiling widely and rubbing my forehead. (Had my often-furrow given me away?)

"Thank you, Jack."

One of my favorite Bible verses is Mark 9:24–"I believe, help thou my unbelief." This is an acknowledgement of faith, a faith that acknowledges its limits. I appreciate this verse because I pray it often.

My prayer for my children is that they have a firm assurance and confidence in Christ. We use the word *hope* too lightly. "I hope I do well on that test" usually is said by someone who has doubts. My children deserve a doubtless hope, a dauntless hope–a definite hope. "Be happy, my children–because there is Jesus."

Lord,

"My hope is built on nothing less than Jesus' blood and righteousness. I dare not trust the sweetest frame, but wholly lean on Jesus' name. On Christ the solid rock I stand, all other ground is sinking sand; all other ground is sinking sand" (Mote).

I pray, with all my heart, for hope that is a solid rock of certainty in the hearts and in the lives of my children, for a "blessed assurance" that becomes the story and the song of their lives (Crosby). I want them to know you, and to know that the sacrifice of your Son means surety and salvation. Let their hope be firm, strong, true—three words that also describe your love.

In every day, in every way, may my children "wholly lean on Jesus' name" (Mote). He will hold them up: may they never fear a fall.

We are so blessed.

Amen.

Heaven

The Word

Thank the Lord that "Earth has no sorrow that Heaven cannot heal" (Thomas Moore 192). This place that is "the abode of God, the angels, and the spirits of the righteous after death; the place or state of existence of the blessed after the mortal life" ("Heaven") will make everything worth it, will be a rest for the righteous weary. "*Heavenly* joys are the fruit of all our labors in this earthly course" (Crabb 385).

We can have blessings here and beyond, as long as our focus is true: "aim at heaven, and you will get earth thrown in. Aim at earth, and you will get neither" (C. S. Lewis).

When all is said and done, what we've said and done will mean all.

The Way

Through Christ-through His self-sacrifice-we have redemption (Ephesians 1:7-8), and in this redemption is an opportunity for Heaven, the place God has set up His throne (Psalm 103:19). This is a place of rejoicing and praise of His holiness, righteousness, and awesomeness! "Praise Him, all His angels; praise Him, all His heavenly hosts" (Psalm 148:2)-this heavenly group of worshipers can one day include us!

I'm sorry for the overuse of exclamation points. I know that William Strunk Jr. and E. B. White would be appalled, but how can I not be excited? Right now I live in an "earthly tent" that can be destroyed, but I know "we have a building from God, and eternal house in heaven, not built by human hands" (2 Corinthians 5:1). I've seen a lot of beautiful architecture in my day, some in person and some only through pictures. But nothing we've created can compare to the dwelling we will one day share with the Great Designer!

The Want

I put this chapter last, because it truly is the finality of my prayer for my children. I want beautiful, blessed lives for them here on earth, but-in the end-what I want more than anything else I could ever ever ever think of is to one day be in heaven with my family. Forever. One day they'll leave my house to go start lives, careers, and families of their own. I want them to visit me often. My heart will be sad in their absences, but our lives here will be short in comparison to our time in eternity.

Lord,

First—I pray you equip me with the words, actions, and behaviors I need to be a solid example of your truth to my children. Let me do everything within my power always to show them of you. I want them to see in me a desire to be yours and to do your will. I want our home to be a haven before heaven.

I want forever-blessings for my children, and that means I want heaven. It is the top, the end, the culmination of everything else I pray for. And in their walk through this journey to the Ultimate Destination, I want to now pray for every part of their being. This is a prayer I started as I would rock my first difficult newborn, trying to focus on prayer instead of self-pity. I lift it up now:

- Please be with their heads—let them KNOW you, and may they often bow their heads in prayer.

- Be with their eyes—I want them to take in the beauty of the world. Let them also see the needs of others, and work in your name to do something about it. And give them discernment in what they see, and in what they chose to see.

- Be with their noses—may they know they are an "aroma of Christ" (2 Corinthians 2:15), an example of Him to others. And may they breathe in the sweetness that is your love.

- Be with their ears—help these ears to hear true "I love you"s throughout their lives. Let them hear honest praise and know they can be confident in these words because of the gifts you have granted them. And may they be sheltered, to some degree, from violent language and rage.

- Be with their mouths—let their mouths praise, uplift, glorify. Do not let them scorn, mock, hurt. May their words amplify that they belong to you. Also, let them savor your Word.

- Be with their necks—may they never feel that Christianity is a heavy yoke to bear, but a beautiful dedication to the Worthy One.

- Be with their shoulders—I pray the

world never rests there. Give them an appropriate amount of responsibilities to themselves, to others, and to you, but let them know they can conquer it in your name.

- Be with their backs—as they do have to carry a heavy burden, give them the strength to do so.

- Be with their hearts—may every beat be a joyful noise, a drumming of love for you (and for their mama). May their hearts be strong, powerful, and full.

- Be with their hands—I pray these hands have many uses in your Kingdom, and that my children will put their hands to work to glorify you. May they know the beauty of touching someone they truly love, of one day holding their own children.

- Be with their stomachs—may they not know hunger, except a holy hunger, unsatiated by anything but you.

- Be with those parts that make them he and she—Lord, I want purity for my children. I pray for fertility and focus, a focus on the fact that their bodies are temples to praise you, not to pleasure themselves outside of your way. May they know the awesome passion in marriage that makes the two into one.

- Be with their rears-get them going in life for you! I pray they have relaxation when necessary, but I pray they aren't habitually lazy.

- Be with their knees-may they be a little calloused in the time spent on the floor in prayer to you.

- Be with their feet, Lord-direct and guide them on the path of life, away from sin and, in the end, into your arms.

I know this was a much longer prayer than the previous ones, but it has reason to be. The end of this book deals with the end of our lives. In the lives of my children, Lord, may everything point to Heaven.

We are so blessed,

and the greatest blessing of all will be when we are with you.

Amen.

Notes

Notes

Questions for Reflection

As you read each chapter, grab a journal and maybe a friend or devotional group. Consider your answers for these questions privately, or share in a time of discussion.

Chapter 1 Phililogia

1. What is a favorite verse from Proverbs?
2. Consider doing an online image or Pinterest search of the word *Proverbs*. Scriptural or not, what is a quote you find that speaks to you?
3. Think of a time you saw your child (or another little one) discover something new. When was the last time you felt the same awe and wonder? How can we keep phililogia active in our own lives?

Chapter 2 Peace

1. Do you consider yourself a peaceful person? Why or why not?

2. Think of someone you know who seems at peace. What is this person like?

3. I often find calm in a cup of hot tea, a good book, or a classic hymn. In what ways do you seek peace in your day?

4. Do you set the value of peace and getting along together as a high standard in your home? Were you raised in a home that promoted peace?

5. How can you begin to instate peace in your home, or how can you continue to teach your children the importance of this quality?

Chapter 3 Purity

1. First Corinthians 6:12-20 is referenced so often that it sometimes loses its intensity. Consider these words: "your body is a temple." Do you treat your body as the holy property of the Most High?

2. Purity can connect with a positive self-image. How can we, as women, model an *appropriate* appreciation of our bodies to our children?

3. How can we raise children who will remain pure in a world where this quality is rare?

Chapter 4 Passion

1. What can we do to model a properly passionate relationship to our children?

2. How do you treat your husband, both in front of the children and when you think they aren't aware? Do you act as a captivating woman he would be quick to cherish?

3. Perhaps your marriage is presently in a state where the passion of your youth is no longer as bright: arguments, incompatibilities, and even exhaustion can get in the way of rejoicing in your love. Spend some time in prayer this week for your own relationship.

4. If you are unmarried, what can you do to show your children the significance of a woman being cherished?

5. Married or unmarried, how can you show your children your faith in the truth that God cherishes you?

Chapter 5 Purpose

1. Do you feel God has a specific purpose (or specific purposes) for you? Have these changed at different phases of your life?

2. What is God calling you to do and be right now?

3. Do you feel equipped to answer this call? How can you become better equipped?

4. How can you model the beauty of living a purposeful life to your children?

5. How can you help your kids find their purpose in life and live their gifts for God?

Chapter 6 Prosperity

1. How do we raise children with a healthy respect of money and materials?

2. Spending habits can make or break secure finances. Are you currently modeling the value of budgeting?

3. Where does money lie on your list of priorities in life? How does this affect your children?

Chapter 7 Perseverance

1. Most likely you are working through something in your life right now that requires perseverance. What and who in your life encourage you to keep pressing on?

2. Do you have a Bible verse you turn to when you need extra encouragement?

3. Write this verse and place in areas where you will see it throughout the day. You can also leave other motivating notes to yourself.

4. We all struggle. Think of a friend who is working through a difficult situation, and reach out with kind words, scripture, a helpful act, or a gift.

Chapter 8 Companionship

1. Are you a good friend? Think of ways you are. Consider ways you could improve.

2. What are qualities you value in a friend?

3. What are qualities you want in the friends of your children?

4. Make it a point this week to connect with at least one of your friends.

Chapter 9 Compassion

1. Would you consider yourself a compassionate person?

2. Is your concern for others just a feeling-or does it move you to action? What are ways you live out compassion for other people?

3. How are you encouraging or how can you encourage your children to bless those in need?

4. Find a service project or charity this week you and your child can work with together. Try to find an organization that relates to your child's interests so he or she will find it easier to make a heart-connection.

Chapter 10 Courage

1. Think of someone in your life who has exhibited great courage. What exactly do you admire about this person?

2. We all have fears; we all worry. Are your fears or worries to the point of inhibiting a trusting relationship with God?

3. If courage isn't the absence of fear, but rather a particular reaction in the face of fear-how does having courage relate to the state of our faith in God?

4. Courage doesn't always bring the obviously measurable success we are used to seeing. How can you praise not only your child's

accomplishments this week, but also his or her efforts?

Chapter 11 Cleverness

1. Do you encourage your child to think critically and solve problems? Are you quick to fix a difficulty because it is often faster and easier that way?

2. Do you tend to undervalue your child's cleverness because it isn't the conventional kind of "smart?" Do you tend to overpraise your child's "smarts" to the point of ignoring other possible giftings-or areas your child wants to excel in that may require more work on his or her part?

3. How can we support our children's strengths and also show them the worth of working through their weaknesses?

4. How can we teach our children to use their strengths to work through their weaknesses?

Chapter 12 Health

1. Remember that verse in 1 Corinthians-"your body is a temple"-it applies here as well. Are you modeling a healthy lifestyle and treating your body with respect?

2. How can you create a home environment that aspires towards holistic health—with care of the mind, body, soul, and spirit?

3. What motivates you to be healthy?

Chapter 13 Humor

1. How often do you laugh during the day? Do you take the time to enjoy the lighter moments of life?

2. If you find yourself too tightly wound or stressed to live in a good sense of humor, how can you bring more (appropriate) hilarities into your life?

Chapter 14 Happiness

1. Are you happy? This minute? In general?

2. What are things that rob you of happiness?

3. Do you think you might be putting too much responsibility on someone or something else to produce your happiness?

4. What brings you true joy?

5. How can you capture joy and live a truly exuberant life?

6. How can we affirm to our children that their presence in our lives brings us joy?

Chapter 15 Hope

1. What is something you hope for?

2. In times of trial, what brings you comfort and helps you lean on Jesus?

3. What is a Bible verse about hope that inspires you?

4. Consider doing an online image or Pinterest search of the word *Hope*. Scriptural or not, what is a quote you find that speaks to you? One of my favorite non-biblical hope quotes is from Emily Dickinson: "Hope is the thing with feathers / That perches in the soul / And sings the tune without the words / And never stops at all" (ll. 1-4).

Chapter 16 Heaven

1. When you were young, do you remember how you pictured heaven? How do your children describe it?

2. How does the knowledge of heaven affect how you treat others?

3. How does the knowledge of heaven affect how you survive trials?

4. How does the knowledge of heaven affect how you raise your children?

Overall

1. Which area / chapter was the hardest for you to think about? Which do you need to work on the most in your own life? Why?

2. Are there particular chapters you feel a stronger need or desire to pray about for each of your children? List each child.

Final Note

"Never let the sense of failure keep you from moving forward with Christ." Oswald Chambers

I am ever-so-far from perfect. This is only one of my stalemate excuses. I can talk myself out of or into almost anything, and any past mistake made feels like a great reason to avoid advancement.

I'm not the right voice. Moses said he wasn't a gifted public speaker, and he questioned God's appointment of him to talk a pharaoh into doing God's will (Exodus 4:10). Since I spent many years as a professor, I don't tell God I'm not good at talking, but that I'm probably not the right one to do the talking. Who wants the girl with raw cookie dough on her breath telling them the importance of nutrition? Yes, I'm trying to be better, but I'm not perfect yet.

I'll speak up when I get to perfect. That way no one will question my authority. That way, God's reputation won't falter based on my failures. Yeah. That's a good idea. Then my life will "so shine before men" (Matthew 5:16) that they'll see the perfect Creator through His perfect creation.

Stop.

I tend to feel I'm not accomplishing *anything* if I'm not mastering *everything*, but, let's face it—I'm human. I'm not perfect. If I keep waiting to do what I feel God is prompting me to do until I feel I have a clean slate...well, I'll be writing my life work in chalk with one hand and furiously erasing with the other, hoping no one has a chance to sneak a peak at my mistakes.

But my mistakes are *everywhere*, ranging from actual physical scars I see every day to emotional ones in my heart or in the hearts of others I've hurt. I can let it keep me back. The devil cannot think of anything that would make him happier.

"Never let the sense of failure keep you from moving forward with Christ." Oswald Chambers

His perfect hand is stretched out, and He's saying to me, "Come on," and to others, "She's with me."

References

Bacon, Francis. "Friends and Friendship." *The Merriam-Webster Dictionary of Quotations*. Springfield, Massachusetts: Merriam-Webster, 1992.

Burke, Edmund. "Prosperity." *Dictionary.com*. n.p. n.d. Web. 14 March 2012.

Chambers, Oswald. *My Utmost for His Highest Journal*. Uhrichsville, Ohio: Barbour Publishing, n.d.

"Clever." *Dictionary.com*. n.p. n.d. Web. 26 May 2012.

"Compassion." *Dictionary.com*. n.p. n.d. Web. 21 April 2012.

"Companionship." *Dictionary.com*. n.p. n.d. Web. 20 April 2012.

Cooley, Mason. "Compassion." *Dictionary.com*. n.p. n.d. Web. 21 April 2012.

Coolidge, Calvin. "Prosperity." *Dictionary.com*. n.p. n.d. Web. 14 March 2012.

Cowley, Abraham. "Hope." *The Merriam-Webster Dictionary of Quotations*. Springfield, Massachusetts: Merriam-Webster, 1992.

Crabb, George. *Crabb's English Synonymes*. New York: Harper & Brothers Publisher, 1917.

Crosby, Fanny J. "Blessed Assurance." *Cyberhymnal.org*. 1873. Web. 14 January 2014.

De Cervantes, Miguel. "Purpose." *The Merriam-Webster Dictionary of Quotations*. Springfield, Massachusetts: Merriam-Webster, 1992.

"The Declaration of Independence." *USHistory.org*. n.p. 4 July 1776. Web. 23 May 2012.

Descartes, Rene. "Intelligence and Intellect." *The Merriam-Webster Dictionary of Quotations*. Springfield, Massachusetts: Merriam-Webster, 1992.

Dickinson, Emily. "Hope is the thing with feathers." *Emily Dickinson: Selected Poems*. Mineola, NY: Dover Publications, 1990. Print.

Eliot, George. "Perseverance." *Dictionary.com*. n.p. n.d. Web. 18 March 2012.

Emerson, Ralph Waldo. "Friends and Friendship." *The Merriam-Webster Dictionary of Quotations*. Springfield, Massachusetts: Merriam-Webster, 1992.

Gary, Romain. "Humor and Wit." *The Merriam-Webster Dictionary of Quotations*. Springfield, Massachusetts: Merriam-Webster, 1992.

"Heaven." *Dictionary.com*. n.p. n.d. Web. 27 May 2012.

Hemingway, Ernest. "Courage." *The Merriam-Webster Dictionary of Quotations*. Springfield, Massachusetts: Merriam-Webster, 1992.

"Hope." *Dictionary.com*. n.p. n.d. Web. 25 May 2012.

Lewis, C. S. "C.S. Lewis Quotes." *Brainyquote.com*. Book Rags Media Network. n.d. Web. 27 May 2012.

Moore, Thomas. "Heaven, Hell, and the Hereafter." *The Merriam-Webster Dictionary of Quotations*. Springfield, Massachusetts: Merriam-Webster, 1992.

Mote, Edward. "My Hope is Built." *Cyberhymnal.org*. Mote's Hymn's of Praise. 1836. Web. 25 May 2012.

Ortega y Gasset, Jose. "Companionship." *The Merriam-Webster Dictionary of Quotations*. Springfield, Massachusetts: Merriam-Webster, 1992.

"Passion." *Dictionary.com*. n.p. n.d. Web. 10 March 2012.

"Peace." *Dictionary.com*. n.p. n.d. Web. 6 March 2012.

"Philologia." *Dictionary.com*. n.p. n.d. Web. 6 Jan. 2012.

Powell, Colin. *Brainyquotes.com*. n.p. n.d. Web. 18 April 2012.

"Purpose." *Dictionary.com*. n.p. n.d. Web. 13 March 2012.

Shakespeare, William. "Courage." *The Merriam-Webster Dictionary of Quotations*. Springfield, Massachusetts: Merriam-Webster, 1992.

Shelley, Mary. "Purpose." *The Merriam-Webster Dictionary of Quotations*. Springfield, Massachusetts: Merriam-Webster, 1992.

Spiderman. Dir. Sam Raimi. Perf. Tobey Maguire and Cliff Robertson. Columbia, 2002. DVD.

Stevenson, Robert Lewis. "Courage." *The Merriam-Webster Dictionary of Quotations*. Springfield, Massachusetts: Merriam-Webster, 1992.

Syrus, Publilus. "Happiness." *The Merriam-Webster Dictionary of Quotations*. Springfield, Massachusetts: Merriam-Webster, 1992.

Twain, Mark. "Courage." "Virtue." *The Merriam-Webster Dictionary of Quotations*. Springfield, Massachusetts: Merriam-Webster, 1992.

Washington, Booker T. *Thinkexist.com*. n.p. n.d. Web. 18 April 2012.

Washington, George. "Virtue." *The Merriam-Webster Dictionary of Quotations*. Springfield, Massachusetts: Merriam-Webster, 1992.

Yeats, W. B. "Friends and Friendship." *The Merriam-Webster Dictionary of Quotations*. Springfield, Massachusetts: Merriam-Webster, 1992.

Yevtushenko, Yevgeny. "Sympathy and Pity." *The Merriam-Webster Dictionary of Quotations*. Springfield, Massachusetts: Merriam-Webster, 1992.

About the Author

I was first published in my elementary school's literary magazine for a rather repetitive poem I wrote about lightning in the 4th grade. The writing bug has had a grip on my immune system ever since.

I work alongside my father/fellow-educator/friend in The Hilliard Institute for Educational Wellness. Our intent is to conduct educational workshops and fundraising events and activities to support local and global non-profit causes and deserving small businesses and individuals. A portion of the profits from the sales of this very book will go to one of the charities we are working with at the time. I delight in my job.

I have previously published five children's books, two textbooks, and one devotional book, co-written with my grandfather and father. I delight in writing.

My writing efforts these days are squeezed in between my educating and wifing and mothering. Married ten years this May 2014, my husband Jay and I have two sons, Jack and Jonas, and a daughter, June, who wasn't yet around as I was writing this book. I delight in my sweet family.

I've taught Bible classes ranging from cradle roll to high school. Hymns, classic devotional books, nature walks, prayers with my family—I delight in my Lord. I write because it draws me nearer to knowing Him, and I hope my reader feels the same on the "other side" of my words.

www.ingramcontent.com/pod-product-compliance
Lightning Source LLC
Chambersburg PA
CBHW061331040426
42444CB00011B/2868

9780991279227